Edmund Goldsmid, Charles Kirkpatrick Sharpe

A Ballad Book - Popular and Romantic Ballads and Congs current in Annandale and Other Parts of Scotland

Part II

Edmund Goldsmid, Charles Kirkpatrick Sharpe

A Ballad Book - Popular and Romantic Ballads and Congs current in Annandale and Other Parts of Scotland
Part II

ISBN/EAN: 9783744774543

Printed in Europe, USA, Canada, Australia, Japan

Cover: Foto ©Thomas Meinert / pixelio.de

More available books at **www.hansebooks.com**

Bibliotheca Curiosa.

A

BALLAD BOOK;

OR,

POPULAR AND ROMANTIC BALLADS AND
SONGS CURRENT IN ANNANDALE AND
OTHER PARTS OF SCOTLAND.

COLLECTED BY

CHARLES KIRKPATRICK SHARPE.

Reprinted from the Rare Original Edition of 1824.

and Edited by

EDMUND GOLDSMID.

———

PART II.

———

PRIVATELY PRINTED, EDINBURGH.

—

1891.

INDEX TO PART II.

A BALLAD BOOK.

XXI.

THE BONNY HOUSE OF AIRLIE

It fell on a day, and a bonny simmer day,
  When green grew aits and barley,
That there fell out a great dispute
  Between Argyll and Airlie.

Argyll has raised an hundred men,
  An hunder harness'd rarely,
And he's awa' by the back of Dunkell,
  To plunder the Castle of Airlie.

Lady Ogilvie looks o'er her bower window
  And oh, but she looks weary ;
And there she spy'd the great Argyll,
  Come to plunder the bonny House of Airlie.

" Come down, come down, my Lady Ogilvie,
  Come down, and kiss me fairly."
" O, I winna kiss the fause Argyll,
  If he should na leave a standing stane in
    Airlie."

He hath taken her by the left shoulder,
  Says, " Dame, where lies thy dowry?"
" Oh, it's east and west yon wan water side,
  And it's down by the banks of the Airlie."

They hae sought it up, they hae sought it down,
  They hae sought it maist severely;
Till they fand it in the fair plumb tree,
  That shines on the bowling-green of Airlie.

He hath taken her by the middle sae small,
  And, O, but she grat sairly:
And laid her down by the bonny burn-side,
  Till they plundered the Castle of Airlie.

" Gif my gude lord war here this night,
  As he is with King Charlie,
Neither you nor ony ither Scottish lord,
  Durst awow to the plundering of Airlie.

" Gif my gude lord war now at hame,
  As he is with his King,
There durst nae a Campbell in a' Argyll,
  Set fit on Airlie green.

"Ten bonny sons I have born unto him,
The eleventh ne'er saw his daddy,
But though I had an hundred mair,
I'd gie them a' to King Charlie."*

XXII.
O, GIN YE WAR DEAD, GUDEMAN.

O, GIN ye war dead, Gudeman,
And a green sod on your heid, Gudeman ;
Then I wad war my widowhood,
Upon a rantin' Highlandman!
There's a sheep's heid in the pat, Gudeman,
A sheep's heid in the pat, Gudeman,
The broo to mee, the horns to thee,
An' the flesh to our John Highlandman.

Chorus.

Sing round about the fire wi' a rung scho ran,
An' round about the fire wi' a rung scho ran,
And round about the fire wi' a rung scho ran,
"Had awa' your blue breeks frae me, Gude-
man."

---

* In the year 1640, Airlie Castle was destroyed by the Marquis of Argyll—a nobleman never accused of incontinence, as might be supposed from this ballad, which is erroneous in another point, at least ; no Lady Ogilvie had eleven sons : the first Earl's wife had three, his daughter-in-law, who is probably the heroine of the song, only one ; she herself was a daughter of Lord Banff.—C. K. S.

This ballad is very common in all parts of Scotland ; innumerable versions have appeared.

XXIII.

THE DREAM.

(*Tune :* " Gramachree.")

LAST night I dreamt my Peggy
　　Was in beneath the bed ;
And up I got upo' my doup,
　　And, oh ! but I was glad.

I pat my hand beneath the bed
　　To tak' her be the lug,
But instead o' my dear Peggy,
　　I gat the water mug ! *

XXIV.

THE CRAB.

OUR gude wife's wi' bairn, and that's of a lad,
And sho's ta'en a greenin' for a fish crab.
　　　　With my hey jing, &c.

Up gat our gudeman, and cleekit to his claithes,
And he's awa' to the sea-side, trippin' on his taes.
　　　　With my hey jing, &c.

---

* The above song used to be sung by a gentleman very eminent at the Scottish Bar, who was born in the year 1680.—C. K. S.

" Have ye ony crab-fish ? "—" One, two, three."
" Tippence is the price o' them gin you and I'll
    agree."
            With my hey jing, &c.

He's pu'd out his purse, and bought the biggest
    ane,
He's put it in his nicht mutch, and he's come
    toddlin' hame.
            With my hey jing, &c.

He wadna put it on the dresser, for fylin' a' the
    dishes,
But he pat it in the chalmer pat, where our gude
    wife——.
            With my hey jing, &c.

Up gat the guid wife, an' for to mak' her dam,
Up gat the crab-fish, and took her be the wame.
            With my hey jing, &c.

Up gat the gudeman, to redd the fish's claws,
Up gat the crab-fish, and took him by the nose.
            With my hey jing, &c.

---

* This gross old ditty is founded on a story in " Le
Moyen de Parvenir," a book of which the extreme wit is
at least equalled by its beastliness.—C. K. S.

XXV.

ANDREW CAR.

Chorus.

HEY for Andrew, Andrew,
Hey for Andrew Car!
He gaed to bed to the lass,
And forgot to bar the door!

Andrew Car is cunnin',
Andrew Car is slee,
And Andrew Car is winnin',
And Andrew Car for me.
    Sing hey for Andrew, &c.

O it was Andrew Car,
O it was him, indeed;
O it was Andrew Car
Wha gat my maidenhead.
    Sing hey for Andrew, &c.

XXVI.

THE HAGGIS O' DUNBAR.

HEY, the Haggis o' Dunbar,
    Fatharalinkum Feedle;
Mony better, few waur,
    Fatharalinkum Feedle.

For to mak' this Haggis nice,
    Fatharalinkum Feedle :
They pat it in a peck o' lice,
    Fatharalinkum Feedle.

For to mak' this Haggis fat,
    Fatharalinkum Feedle ;
They put in a scabbit cat,
    Fatharalinkum Feedle.

    *   *   *   *   *

XXVII.

THE BONNY LAD.

HE's a bonny, bonny lad that's a courting me,
He's a bonny, bonny lad that's a courting me ;
He's cripple of a leg, and blind of an e'e,
He's a bonny, bonny lad that's a courting me !

    *   *   *   *   *

XXVIII.

FAIR MARGARET OF CRAIGNARGAT.

FAIR Margaret of Craignargat
    Was the flow'r of all her kin,
And she's fallen in love with a false young man,
    Her ruin to begin.

The more she lov'd, the more it prov'd
    Her fatal destiny ;
And he that sought her overthrow,
    Shar'd of her misery.

Before that lady she was born,
    Her mother, as we find,
She dreamt she had a daughter fair,
    That was both dumb and blind.

But as she sat in her bow'r door,
    A viewing of her charms,
There came a raven from the south,
    And pluck'd her from her arms.

Three times on end she dreamt this dream,
    Which troubled sore her mind,
That from that very night and hour,
    She could no comfort find.

Now she has sent for a wise woman,
    Liv'd nigh unto the port,
Who being call'd, instantly came,
    That lady to comfort.

To her she told her dreary dream,
    With salt tears in her eye;
Hoping that she would read the same,
    Her mind to satisfy.

"Set not your heart on children young,
    Whate'er their fortune be,
And if I tell what shall befall,
    Lay not the blame on me.

" The raven which you dreamed of,
   He is a false young man,
With subtile heart and flatt'ring tongue,
   Your daughter to trepan.

" Both night and day, 'tis you I pray
   For to be on your guard,
For many are the subtile wyles,
   By which youth are ensnar'd."

When she had read the dreary dream,
   It vexed her more and more,
For Craignargat of birth and state,
   Liv'd nigh unto the shore.

But as in age her daughter wax'd,
   Her beauty did excel
All the ladies far and near,
   That in that land did dwell.

The Gordon, Hay, and brave Agnew,
   Three knights of high degree,
Unto the dame a courting came,
   All for her fair beauty.

Which of these men they asked her then,
   That should her husband be ?
But scornfully she did reply,
   " I'll wed none of the three."

" Since it is so, where shall we go,
   A match for thee to find?
Thou art so fair and beautiful,
   That none can suit thy mind."

With scorn and pride she answer made,
   " You'll ne'er choice one for me,
Nor will I wed against my mind,
   For all their high degree."

The brave Agnew, whose heart was true,
   A solemn vow did make,
Never to love a woman more,
   All for that lady's sake.

To counsel this lady was deaf,
   To judgment she was blind,
Which griev'd her tender parents dear
   And troubled sore their mind.

From the Isle of Man a courter came,
   And a false young man was he,
With subtile heart and flatt'ring tongue,
   To court this fair lady.

This young man was a bold outlaw,
   A robber and a thief,
But soon he gain'd this lady's heart,
   Which caused all their grief.

"O, will you wed," her mother said,
  "A man you do not know,
For to break your parents' heart,
  With shame but and with woe?"

"Yes, I will go with him," she said,
  "Either by land or sea,
For he's the man I've pitched on,
  My husband for to be."

"O, let her go," her father said,
  "For she shall have her will.
My curse and mallison she's get,
  For to pursue her still."

"Your curse, father, I don't regard,
  Your blessing I'll ne'er crave;
To the man I love, I'll constant prove,
  And never him deceive."

On board with him fair Marg'ret's gone,
  In hopes his bride to be.
But mark you well, and I shall tell
  Of their sad destiny.

They had not sail'd a league but five,
  Till the storm began to rise;
The swelling seas ran mountains high,
  And dismal were the skies.

B

In deep despair, that lady fair,
  For help aloud she cries,
While crystal tears, like fountains ran
  Down from her lovely eyes.

" O ! I have got my father's curse,
  My pride for to subdue ;
With sorrows great my heart will break,
  Alas ! what shall I do ?

" O, were I at my father's house,
  His blessing to receive,
Then on my bended knees I'd fall
  His pardon for to crave.

" To aid my grief, there's no relief,
  To speak it is in vain,
Likewise my loving parents dear,
  I ne'er shall see again."

The wind and waves did both conspire,
  The lives for to devour,
The gallant ship that night was lost,
  And never was seen more.

When tidings to Craignargat came,
  Of their sad overthrow,
It griev'd her tender parents' heart,
  Afresh began their woe.

Of the dreary dream that she had seen,
    And often thought upon,
" O fatal news," her mother cries,
    " My darling, she is gone !

" O fair Marg'ret, I little thought,
    The seas should be thy grave,
When first thou left thy father's house,
    Without thy parents' leave."

May this tragedy a warning be,
    To children while they live,
That they may love their parents dear,
    Their blessing to receive.*

---

* Craignargat is a promontory in the bay of Luce. Although almost surrounded by the Barony of Mochrum, it was long possessed by a branch of the family of Macdowall, which was probably our heroine's surname. On the head of Fair Margaret's lovers, it may be remarked that the Agnews of Lochnaw are a very ancient family, and hereditary Sheriffs of Wigton. The Gordon mentioned was probably Gordon of Craighlaw, whose castle was situated about five miles from Craignargat, in the parish of Kirkcowan, considered so remote before the formation of military roads, that the local proverb says, "Out of the world and into Kirkcowan." The Hays of Park dwelt on the coast, about six miles from Craignargat ; but it is singular that the lady is not complimented with a Dunbar as her lover, the Place of Mochrum, as the old tower is called, being only two miles from her reputed residence.—C. K. S.

This ballad, according to Motherwell, was a common stall ballad, about 1760.

XXIX.
KEMPY KAYE.

KEMPY KAYE's a wooing gane,
  Far, far ayont the sea,
An' he has met with an auld auld man,
  His gudefather to be.

" Gae scrape yeersel, and gae scart yeersel,
  And mak your bruchty face clean,
For the wooers are to be here the nicht,
  And yeer body's to be seen.*

" What's the matter wi' you, my fair maiden,
  You look so pale and wan?
I'm sure you was once the fairest maiden,
  That ever the sun shined on."

Sae they scrapit her, and they scartit her,
  Like the face of any assy pan ;
And in cam Kempy Kaye himself,
  A clever and tall young man.

His teeth they were like tether sticks,
  His nose was three feet lang ;
Between his shouthers was ells three,
  Between his een a span.

---

* Var. Kempy Kaye's to be here the nicht,
  Or else the morn at een.—C. K. S.

"I'm coming to court your dochter dear,
  An' some pairt of your gear."
An' by my sooth," quo' Bengoleer,
  "She'll sair a man o' weir."

"My dochter she's a thrifty lass,
  She span seven year to me,
An' if it war weil counted up,
  Full ten wobs it would be."

He led his dochter by the han,
  His dochter ben brought he;
"O, is not she the fairest lass,
  That's in great Christendye?"

Ilka hair intil her head,
  Was like a heather cow,
And ilka louse aninder it,
  Was like a lintseed bow.*

She had lauchty teeth an' kaily lips,
  An' wide lugs fu' o' hair;
Her pouches fu' o' pease meal daigh,
  War hinging down her spare.

Ilka ee intil her head,
  Was like a rotten ploom,
An' down down browit was the quean,
  An' sairly did she gloom.

---

* Var. Was like a brucket yowe.

22 A BOOK OF BALLADS.

Ilka nail upon her hand,
  Was like an iron rake,
An' ilka teeth into her head,
  Was like a tether stake.

She gied to him a gay gravat,
  O' the auld horse's sheet,
And he gied her a gay gold ring,
  O' the auld couple reet.*

XXX.

THE PUDDY AND THE MOUSE.

THERE lived a puddy in a well,
And a merry mouse in a mill.

Puddy he'd a wooin' ride,
Sword and pistol by his side.

---

* *i.e.* root.—C. K. S.

This song my learned readers will perceive to be of
Scandinavian origin ; and that the wooer's name was probably suggested by Sir Kayes of the Round Table, whose
lady failed to prove her chastity in the troublesome affair
of the mantle. The description of Bengoleer's daughter
resembles that of the enchanted damsel who appeared to
courteous King Henrie.

N.B.—This and the following ballad should have been
placed much earlier in the series.—C. K. S.

Puddy cam to the mouse's wonne,
" Mistress Mouse, are you within ? "

" Yes, kind sir, I am within,
Saftly do I sit and spin."

" Madame, I am come to woo,
Marriage I must have of you."

" Marriage I will grant you nane,
Till Uncle Rotten he comes hame."

" Uncle Rotten's now come hame,
Fye gar busk the bride alang."

Lord Rotten sat at the head o' the table,
Because he was baith stout and able.

Wha is't that sits next the wa',
But Lady Mouse baith jimp and sma' ?

Wha is't that sits next the bride,
But the sola puddy wi' his yellow side ? *

Syme cam the dewk but and the drake,
The dewk took the puddy and gart him squaik.

---

* Var. Wha sat at the table fit,
     Wha but froggy and his lame fit ?—C. K. S.

Than cam in the carle cat,
Wi' a fiddle on his back ;
" Want ye ony music here?" *

The puddy he swam down the brook,
The drake he catch'd him in his fluke.

The cat he pu'd Lord Rotten down,
The kittlens they did claw his crown.

But Lady Mouse baith jimp and sma',
Crept into a hole beneath the wa' ;
" Squeak," quo' she, " I'm weel awa'." †

---

* Var. Then in cam the gude grey cat,
    Wi' a' the kittlens at her back.—C. K. S.

† Among the songs enumerated in the·" Complainte of Scotland " (1594) is, " The frog cam to the myl dur," probably founded on the same legend with this, which has a chorus, " Cuddie alone and I," &c., not worthy of insertion. In November, 1580, the Stationers licensed to E. White " A ballad of a most strange wedding of the frogge and the mouse," which has since frequently appeared in a more modern shape. See also in D'Urffey's Pills, vol. v., " A ditty on a high amour at St. James's; the words by Mr. D'Urffey, and set to a comical tune."—C. K. S.

XXXI.
THE EARL OF ERROL.

O ERROL it's a bonny place,
    It stands in yonder glen ;
The lady lost the rights of it,
    The first night she gaed hame.

Chorus.

    A waly, and a waly,
        According as ye ken ;
    The thing we ca' the ranting o't
        Our Lady lies her lane, O !

" What need I wash my apron,
    Or hing it on yon door,
What need I truce my petticoat,
    It hangs even down before ? "
        A waly, &c.

Errol's up to Edinburgh gaen,
    That bonny burrows town !
He has chused the Barber's daughter,
    The toss of a' that town.
        A waly, &c.

He's ta'en her by the milk-white hand,
    He's led her o'er the green,
And twenty times he kist her,
    Before his Lady's een.
        A waly, &c.

" Look up, look up, now Peggy,
    Look up and think nae shame,
  For I'll give thee five hundred pound,
    To buy to thee a gown ! "
        A waly, &c.

" Look up, look up, now Peggy,
    Look up and think nae shame ;
  For I'll gie thee five hundred pound,
    To bear to me a son."
        A waly, &c.

" Your name is Kate Carnegie,
    And I'm Sir Gilbert Hay ;
  I'll gar your father sell his lands,
    Your tocher gude to pay."
        A waly, &c.

Now he may take her back again,
    Do wi' her what he can,
  For Errol canna please her,
    Nor ane o' a' his men.
        A waly, &c.

" Go fetch to me a pint of wine,
    Go fill it to the brim ;
  That I may drink my gude Lord's health,
    Tho' Errol be his name."
        A waly, &c.

She has ta'en the glass into her hand,
  She has putten poison in;
She has sign'd it to her dorty lips,
  But ne'er a drop went in.
    A waly, &c.

Up then spak a little page,
  He was o' Errol's kin,
" Now fie upon ye, lady gay,
  There's poison there within."
    A waly, &c.

" It's hold your hand now, Kate," he says,
  " Hold it back again,
For Errol shall not drink on't,
  Nor none of all his men."
    A waly, &c.

She has taen the sheets into her arms,
  She has thrown them o'er the wa';
" Since I maun gae maiden hame again,
  Awa', Errol, awa'."
    A waly, &c.

She's down the back o' the garden,
  And O ! as she did murne !
" How can a warkman crave his wage,
  When he never wrought a turn ?"

A waly and a waly,
   According as ye ken ;
The thing we ca' the ranting o't,
Our Lady lies her lane, O ! *

XXIII.
RICHIE STORIE.

THE Earl o' Wigton had three daughters,
O braw wallie ! but they were bonnie ;
The youngest o' them, and the bonniest too,
Has fallen in love wi' Richie Storie.

---

* The following extract from a letter addressed by Keith, of Benholm, to Captain Brown, at Paris, explains the subject of this ballad, which was preserved by the peasantry of Annandale, probably owing to the circumstance of Lord Southesque, Lady Errol's brother, being at one time possessor of Hoddam Castle : " You may have heard ere this of Glencairne's marriage with the Countess Dowager of Tweddell, mother-in-lawe to your cousin ; and what accessione of French landes Glencairne's son is lyke to bring to his familie, by a cadet of their hous and name, a French marquis, who hath carried my Lord Kilmaurs and his brother to France for that effect.   Then the death of your cousin's lady, my Lady Wigtoune ; with that of the Erll of Annandell, Bauvaird by his death becoming Viscount Stormont and Lord Scoon.   Lastly, the sadd (and not lyke heard of in this land amongst eminent persons) story of the Erll of Erroll's impotencie, which is lyke, being cum to publick hearing, to draw deeper betwix him and Southesk, than is alledgit it hath done 'twixt him and Southesk's daughter.   These are the meane emergents we are taken up with, whilst beyond sea empyres are overturning. Scoone, 22d. Feb., 1659."—C.K.S.

See also a version in Maidment's " North Countrie Garland."

" Here's a letter for ye, madame,
Here's a letter for ye, madame,
The Erle o' Home wad fain presume,
To be a suitor to ye, madame."

" I'l hae nane o' your letters, Richie,
I'l hae nane o' your letters, Richie,
For I've made a vow, and I'l keep it true,
That I'l have none but you, Ritchie."

" O do not say so, madame,
O do not say so, madame,
For I have neither land nor rent,
For to maintain you o', madame.

" Ribands ye maun wear, madame,
Ribands ye maun wear, madame,
With the bands about your neck,
O' the goud that shines sae clear, madame."

" I'l lie ayont a dyke, Richie,
I'l lie ayont a dyke, Richie,
And I'l be aye at your command,
And bidding whan ye like, Richie."

O, he's gane on the braid, braid road,
And she's gane through the broom sae bonnie,
Her silken robes down to her heels,
And she's awa' wi' Richie Storie.

This lady gade up the Parliament stair,
Wi' pendles in her lugs sae bonnie,
Mony a lord lifted his hat,
But little did they ken she was Richie's lady.

Up then spak the Erle o' Home's lady,
"Was na ye richt sorrie, Annie,
To leave the lands o' bonnie Cumbernauld,
And follow Richie Storie, Annie?"

"O, what need I be sorrie, madame,
O, what need I be sorrie, madame,
For I've got them that I like best,
And war ordained for me, madame!"

"Cumbernauld is mine, Annie,
Cumbernauld is mine, Annie,
And a' that's mine, it shall be thine,
As we sit at the wine, Annie."*

---

* John, third Earl of Wigtown, had six sons and three daughters. The second, Lady Lillias Fleming, was so indiscreet as to marry a footman, by whom she had issue. She and her husband assigned her provision to Lieutenant-Colonel John Fleming, who discharged her renunciation, dated in October, 1673.—C. K. S.

This ballad was sung to the tune of "Braw lads o' Gala Water.

XXXIII.

THE RAPE OF ARNGOSK. (A Fragment.)*

THE Highlandmen hae a' come down,
They've a come down almost,
They've stowen away the bonnie lass,
The Lady of Arngosk.

* This fragment I cannot illustrate, either from history or tradition. Sir William Murray, third son of Sir William Murray of Tullibardine, married Margaret Barclay, the beiress of Arngosk and Kippo, in the reign of King James IV.; but it is very unlikely that the ballad alludes to that match, particularly as it is remembered to have concluded with the lady's restoration to her friends, a *finale* not uncommon in such cases, with which, by the way, our Scottish annals abound.—Ex. grat. A.D. 1336, Allan of Winton forcibly carried off the young beiress of Seton; this produced a feud in Lothian, some favouring the ravisher, while others sought to bring him to punishment. Fordun says, that on this occasion an hundred ploughs in Lothian were laid aside from labour. Master Bowy, in his very curious MS. History of the House of Glenurquhay, informs us that "John Mackrom Macalaster M'Gregor, in anno ——, ravischit Helene Campbell, dochtir to Sir Colene Campbell of Glenurquhay, Knicht. This Helene Campbell was widow, and Lady of Lochbuy, and she was ravischit. The foresaid John was not richteous air to the M'Gregor, but was principal of the clan Donlogneir." Sir Colin, "wha departit this lyfe in the Tour of Straphillane, 24th Sept., 1480," understanding that his daughter had become reconciled to her forced marriage, waylaid his son-in-law at the hill of Drummond, slew him, and cutting off his head, put it into a basket, and covered it with apples. This, as an acceptable present, he sent to his daughter by a messenger, charged not to mention what was concealed at the bottom. In the pedigree of the clan Gregor, it is said that Malcolm M'Gregor *married the lady with a view to conciliate the*

Behind her back they've tied her hands,
An' then they set her on—
" I winna gang wi' you," she said,
" Nor ony Highland loon."

     *   *   *   *   *   *

---

differences between the two families, and that she composed
a mournful song upon his death, which is still preserved :
probably the very ditty now attributed to Rob Roy's widow.
Bothwell's violence to Queen Marie is well known. In the
year 1591, Lord Fountainhall notes from the Criminal
Records of Edinburgh, "Dame Jean Ramsay, Lady
Warriston (she was of the house of Dalheusy), and Advo·
cate, *contra* Robert Carncroce, called Meikle Rob, and
others, for ravishing of her in March last, contrare to the
Acts of Parliament." 1594, " the 14th of August, Christian
Johnstoun, ane widow in Edinburgh, revest by Patrick
Aikenhead. The towne wes put in ane grate fray be the
ringing of the common bell; the said Christiane was
followit and brocht back fra him, sua that the said Patrick
got no advantage of her."—*Birrell's Diary*. In the year
1680, Patrick Carnegie, son to the Earl of Northesk, carried
off by force from the house of Pilcoye, Mary Gray, heiress
of Ballegerno, a child not quite eleven years of age. She
was recovered by her friends fifteen days after. The last
case I shall mention is from Fountainhall : " January 7th,
1688, James Boswell, in Kinghorn, brother to Balmuto, is
pursued by Anna Carmichael, for ravishing her out of her
father's house, and wounding her father, and carrying her
to the Queensferry, where she was rescued ; and being
absent, he is declared fugitive, whereon his escheat falls."
It may be added that in Fountainhall's MS. is the following
curious notice concerning Lord Stormont, descended from
the heiress of Arngosk : " About this tyme (June, 1668) was
given in a bill to the Lords of Secret Counsell complaining
on my Lord Stormond for fraudulent abstracting of Gibson,
the Laird of Durie's niece, to whom the custodie of her
person in law belongeth ; and for being art and part thereof,

XXXIV.
MALCOLM OF BALBEDIE.

BALBEDIE has a second son,
  They ca' him Michael Malcolm,
He gangs about Balgonie dykes,
  Huntin' and hawkin';
He's stowen awa' the bonnie lass,
  An' kept the widow wakin'.*

XXXV.
I HAVE BEEN AT NEWBURN.

I HAVE been at Newburn, I was in the tower,
I have been in Scotland with a royal power,
I have been with Gilbert, and Marg'ret Kennedy,
But such a huffing parliament did I never see!

Thou shalt get a night-cap and a mourning ring,
And to kepp thy head, thy friends a cloth shall
    bring,
And in a wooden casement thy head shall be
    bound,
But thy lusty corpse must stink above the ground.

by accession either antecedent, concomitant, or subsequent.
This bill was given in by Durie, and after a long
dispute, the wholle resulting on my Lord Stormond's oath,
he denied all accession thereto, though it was strongly
soupçouned he was not free."—C. K. S.

  * Malcolm of Balbedie appears to have been a cadet of
the Lochor family, whose representative was created a
Baronet of Nova Scotia in the year 1665. I do not know
the anecdote on which this fragment was composed.—
C.K.S.

C

Thou shalt be conducted from Thames to Tweed-
    side,
Like a malefactor thy feet shall be tyed,
And from that scurvy process the lawyers shall
    be free,
Thou thought to catch these men, but we have
    catcht thee.*

XXXVI.
TO LAUDERDALE.

LAUDERDALE, what has become
    Of all thy former huffing,
Has the Commons struck thee dumb,
    And sent thee thus a snuffing?
Or is it that the late address
For removing thee and Bess,
        Does vex thee? &c.

Since the kingdoms thou must quit,
    And seek new habitation,
Will not thy proud Grace think fit
    T' erect a new plantation?
And since thou now begins to reel,
Pray thee go to Old Brazile,
        And lord it, &c.

---

* This and the following song allude to some political
misfortunes of the Duke of Lauderdale, in the year 1675,
which are well known to every reader of history. Gilbert
is Dr. Burnet, and Margaret, Lady Margaret Kennedy,
his wife.—C.K.S.

XXXVII.

ANNIE LAURIE.

MAXWELTON banks are bonnie,
Whare early fa's the dew;
Whare me and Annie Laurie
Made up the promise true;
Made up the promise true,
And never forget will I,
And for bonnie Annie Laurie
I'd lay down my head and die.

She's backit like a peacock,
She's breastit like a swan,
She's jimp about the middle,
Her waist ye weill may span;
Her waist you weill may span,
And she has a rolling eye,
And for bonnie Annie Laurie
I'd lay down my head and die.*

---

* Sir Robert Laurie, first baronet of the Maxwelton family (created 27th March, 1685), by his second wife, a daughter of Riddell of Minto, had three sons and four daughters, of whom Annie was much celebrated for her beauty, and made a conquest of Mr. Douglas of Fingland, who is said to have composed these verses—under an unlucky star, for the lady afterwards married Mr. Ferguson of Craigderroch.

XXXVIII.

FY, FY, MARG'RET.

(*Tune:* "How are ye, Kimmer?")

"Fy, fy, Marg'ret are ye in?
I nae sooner heard it than I did rin,
Down the gate to tell ye, down the gate to tell
      ye,
Down the gate to tell ye, we'll no be left the skin.

Weel might I kent a' was nae richt,
For I dreamt o' red and green a' the last nicht;
And twa cats fechtin, and twa cats fechtin,
And twa cats fechtin, I waken'd wi' the fricht.

Fare ye weel, woman, I maun rin,
Trew ye, gif our neighbour Eppie be in,
And auld Robie Barber, and auld Robbie Barber,
And auld Robbie Barber, for I maun tell him.

"Bide a wee, woman, and gies't a' out—
They're bringing in black Papary, I doubt, I
      doubt,
And sad reformation, sad reformation,
Sad reformation in a' the kirks about.

Mickle do they say, and mair do we hear,
The Frenches and the Irishes are a' coming here,
And we'll be a' murder'd, murder'd, murder'd,
We'll a' be murder'd, before the new year."

XXXIX.

𝔄 𝔅𝔞𝔩𝔩𝔞𝔡, 𝔅𝔢𝔦𝔫𝔤 𝔱𝔥𝔢 𝔗𝔯𝔲𝔢 ℭ𝔞𝔰𝔢 𝔬𝔣 𝔐𝔯𝔰. 𝔈𝔩𝔰𝔭𝔢𝔱, 𝔞 𝔏𝔞𝔡𝔶'𝔰 𝔊𝔢𝔫𝔱𝔩𝔢𝔴𝔬𝔪𝔞𝔫, 𝔫𝔢𝔞𝔯 𝔈𝔡𝔦𝔫𝔟𝔲𝔯𝔤𝔥.

LANG hae I lo'ed the blate Mass John,
  And sair my breast has smarted ;
I never saw a Dominie
  Was half sae cruel-hearted !

With pleasing words I feast his ears,
  With dainty food I fill him ;
I would not take the Chamberlain,
  But that did naething till him !

When he was with the toothache fash'd,
  I bled his gums with leeches ;
To keep him warm, I sewed mysel',
  Three buttons on his breeches.

I lo'e him in a lawful way,
  No lawful love is wicked ;
I ne'er set on the succar pan,
  But he got aye a lick o't.

Whene'er my dearie would came in,
  The door was never lockit ;
Nor wanted he for a la creesh,
  And seed-cake in his pocket.

I cut the phlegm with Athole brose,
  When cauld did quite confound him ;
I gave him wangrace in his bed,
  And row'd the blankets round him.

With darning his auld coarsest sarks,
  I scarce have left a thumb on ;
But sae I should, for chaplains used
  To love the gentlewoman.

But tho' he reads the Bible book,
  It makes but sma' impression ;
Indeed, he catch'd the cook with Kate,
  And sent them to the Session.

They did not well in what they did,
  So ill the matter ended ;
But lawful love's another thing,
  And ought to be commended.

With comfort met we should delight,
  Mankind should not miscarry ;
But he, for all that I can do,
  Will neither burn nor marry.

Hoot, fye for shame—be brisk, Mass John,
  Ye look as ye were sleepin' ;
Ye craw not like a stately fowl,
  But cackle like a capon.

Oh, dour, Mass John—oh, dreigh, Mass John,
 When I have told you sae far !
A shame light on your loggerhead,
 Ye doited, donnart, duffar ! *

XL.

THE DISTRAUGHT GUDE WIFE.

(*Tune :* "O London is a Fine Town.")

WAS ever dame in such distress?
 My heart is full of care ;
Such various plagues torment my mind,
 That I am in despair.

I'm on and off, and off and on,
 And know not what to do ;
I have a cook to dress my meat,
 But I want to get me two.

This cook a handy damsel is,
 And dresses very weel,
Her kitchen is as clean's her face,
 And her pewther shines like steel.

---

* This and the following ballad were written by Charles
Lord Binning, who died in the lifetime of his father, the
Earl of Haddington, 1733. (See Park's edition of Wal-
pole's "Royal and Noble Authors, vol. v.)

But she has no experience,
   And has so little seen,
That when I want variety,
   She kills me with the spleen.

I have a man cook in my view,
   To help her out a dish,
That when she is employ'd with meat,
   The lad may dress the fish.

But then the lad a head cook is,
   And second will not be ;
I must pack off the lass, I fear,
   For I can't afford her fee.

But then the lass has done no fault—
   I'll keep her, I'm resolved—
I'll get the man to give her half,
   And so the doubt is solv'd.

But what if they should not agree—
   They will my victuals spoil ;
He'll say 'tis her, and she 'tis him,
   And plague me with turmoil.

I'll oot have him, and part with her,
   And yet I'll have him too ;
I'll part with he—no, no, I won't—
   O stars, what shall I do?

XLI.

COLD SIR PETER.

Oh, wherefor did I cross the Forth,
　And leave my love behind me,
Why did I venture to the north,
　With one that does not mind me?

Had I but visited Carin!
　It would have been much better,
Than pique the prudes, and make a din,
　For careless, cold, Sir Peter!

I'm sure I've seen a better limb,
　And twenty better faces;
But still my mind it ran on him,
　When I was at the races.

At night when we went to the ball,
　Were many there discreeter;
The well-bred Dyke,* and lively Maule,
　Panmure behav'd much better.

They kindly show'd their courtesy,
　And look'd on me much sweeter,
Yet easy could I never be,
　For thinking on Sir Peter.

---

* The Duke of Hamilton.

D

I fain would wear an easy air,
  But, oh ! it look'd affected ;
And e'en the fine Ambassador,*
  Could see he was neglected.

Tho' Poury left for me the spleen,
  My temper grew no sweeter ;
I think I'm mad,—what do I mean?
  To follow cold Sir Peter ! †

XLII.

BALMANNO.

WHAT charms can English Margaret boast
  To fix thy inconstant mind,
And keep the heart that I have lost?
  O, cruel and unkind !

---

* The Earl of Stair.

† This and the following songs were composed by Annie, daughter of Sir James Mackenzie, Bart., a Senator of the College of Justice, bearing the title of Lord Royston. She is said to have inherited the wit of her grandfathers, the first Earl of Cromarty, and Sir George Mackenzie, of Rosehaugh, which in some cases overbalanced her discretion. Her lampoons excited as much hatred as mirth, and she met with those spiteful returns which such poetesses must ever expect. This lively lady had no children by her husband, Sir William Dick, of Prestonfield, Bart., and died in the year 1741. Her Phaon, whom she seems to laugh at in these verses, was Sir Patrick Murray, of Balmanno.—C.K.S.

For I can kilt my coats as high,
　And curl my red toupee——
And I'll put on the English mutch,
　If that has charms for thee.

Let no nymph toss thy leathern fan,
　Nor damsel 'touch thy box ;
For I'll, Balmanno, have thee all,
　Even take thee with a . . . !

Since that's, alas ! thy woful case,
　There's none so fit as I ;
For ne'er a lass in all the land,
　Can boast more mercury.*

XLIII.

MRS. MITCHELL AND BORLAN.

" Who's that at my chamber door ? "
　" It's I, my dear," quo' Borlan ;
" Come in," quo' she, " let's chat awhile,
　You strapping, sturdy Norlan."

------

* Written after a raffle, in which Sir Patrick gained a fan
and a snuff-box.　English Margaret was Lady Margaret
Montgomerie, daughter to the Earl of Eglintoune, and
afterwards the wife of Sir James Macdonald, of Slate.　She
is termed English, because she was educated at a boarding-
school near London.—C. K. S.

Fair Mitchell needed add no more,
　For Borlan straight did enter,
And on his knees he vow'd and swore,
　For her he all would venture.

Fair Mitchell answer'd with a blush,
　" Your love I don't intrust, sir,
But should it reach my father's ear,
　How would he puff and bluster ! "

" O, let him bluster as he will,"
　Replied the amorous lover ;
" If you'll consent my arms to fill,
　Let him go to Hanover."*

---

* From circumstances, I suspect this song to be the composition of Lady Dick, but am not certain.

THE END.

www.ingramcontent.com/pod-product-compliance
Lightning Source LLC
Chambersburg PA
CBHW021441090426
42739CB00009B/1577